Lon2 Aa

C000088839

To:

Eileen

From:

Elizabeth

Date:

May 2014

For your 90th Birthday,
with much love,

My heart rejoices and I'm thankful, too,
That I could share this book with you,
For all my poems are woven of
Words I borrow from our Father above ...

IT'S ME AGAIN, LORD

HELEN STEINER RICE

It's me again, Lord contains excerpts from *A book of prayer,* first
published by Fleming H. Revell, a division of Baker Book House
Company, PO Box 6287, Grand Rapids, MI 49516-6287

© 1995 by Virginia J. Ruehlmann and
The Helen Steiner Rice Foundation
Compiled by Virginia J. Ruehlmann

First edition published in South Africa by Christian Art Publishers
PO Box 1599, Vereeniging, 1930
© 1996

Second edition © 2000 by Christian Art Gifts

Cover designed by Christian Art Gifts

Printed and bound in Hong Kong

ISBN 1-86852-604-6

00 01 02 03 04 05 06 07 08 09 · 10 9 8 7 6 5 4 3 2 1

Contents

The Helen Steiner Rice Foundation

God knows no strangers, He loves us all,
The poor, the rich, the great, the small.
He is a Friend who is always there
To share our troubles and lessen our care.
No one is a stranger in God's sight,
For God is love and in His Light
May we, too, try in our small way
To make new friends from day to day.

Whatever the celebration, whatever the day, whatever the event, whatever the occasion, Helen Steiner Rice possessed the ability to express the appropriate feeling for that particular moment in time.

A happening became happier, a sentiment more sentimental, a memory more memorable because of her deep sensitivity to put into understandable language the emotion being experienced. Her positive attitude, her concern for others, and her love of God are identifiable threads woven into her life, her work ... and even her death.

Prior to her passing, she established the

Helen Steiner Rice Foundation, a nonprofit corporation whose purpose is to award grants to worthy charitable programs that aid the elderly, the needy, and the poor. In her lifetime, these were the individuals about whom Mrs. Rice was greatly concerned.

Royalties from the sale of this book will add to the financial capabilities of the *Helen Steiner Rice Foundation*, thus making possible additional grants to various qualified, worthwhile, and charitable programs. Because of her foresight, her caring, and her deep convictions, *Helen Steiner Rice* continues to touch a countless number of lives. Thank you for your assistance in helping to keep Helen's dream alive.

Virginia J. Ruehlmann, Administrator
The Helen Steiner Rice Foundation
Suite 2100, Atrium Two
221 E. Fourth Street
Cincinnati, Ohio 45201

Introduction

Prayer is a magnificent and generous gift from our Father. It is also a conversation, a relationship, a communication with God, initiated by the individual or group doing the praying. Prayer can be

silent or audible,
spontaneous or formal,
memorized or extemporaneous,
expressed privately or
with other members of a family,
church, or organization,
said or sung in a secluded location,
or walking on a crowded street,
while driving or riding in a car, dining or
drifting off to sleep.

Anytime and anywhere is a place for prayer. A prayer can be a form of adoration or praise,

an expression of love and loyalty,
appreciation and thanksgiving,
celebration or consolation, a petition,
a statement of contrition,

a plea for forgiveness or a request for guidance. Prayers can be simply or elaborately stated.

The important characteristics include
the qualities of humility, fidelity, faith,

trust, and sincerity.

Simple, direct, and honest supplications
are heard as clearly
as loquacious and embellished pontifications.

There are no boundaries as to what to pray
for –

one should feel free to take everything
to God in prayer.

The challenge is not only in taking
a concern to Him but
trusting in God's answer and the timing
of His response.

Prayer offers a renewal and revitalization of
spirit and hope.

It is not as important to physically kneel
in prayer but rather to have one's spirit
bow in an attitude of respect.

One's prayer life should be an ongoing pro-
cess,

continuing to become ever more meaning-
ful,

ever more helpful, as

it progresses onward toward the eternal
goal.

Helen Steiner Rice knew the value of a con-
sistent prayerful life and expressed such in
many of her poems. May this collection assist
you in developing and following your own
prayer life.

Prayerfully,
–Virginia J. Ruehlmann –

The meaning
of prayer

He was praying in a certain place.
When he had finished, one of his
disciples asked him, "Lord, teach us to
pray, as John taught his disciples."

~ Luke 11:1 NAB ~

Helen Steiner Rice writes that "prayer is the up-lifting of the heart to God." Catechisms and dictionaries define prayer in a variety of ways ranging from "an offering up of our personal desires to God for things to which He agrees," to "an act of entreating God for certain requests that are important to the one doing the praying." Dwight Eisenhower expressed it this way: "Personal prayer ... is ... as basic to the individual as sunshine, food, and water. A thousand experiences have convinced me beyond room of doubt that prayer multiplies the strength of the individual and brings within the scope of his capabilities almost any conceivable objective."

Not to seek,
Lord, but to share

Dear God, much too often
  we seek You in prayer
Because we are wallowing
  in our own self-despair.
We make every word
  we lamentingly speak
An imperative plea
  for whatever we seek.
We pray for ourselves
  and so seldom for others –
We're concerned with our problems
  and not with our brothers.
We seem to forget, Lord,
  that the sweet hour of prayer
Is not for self-seeking
  but to place in Your care
All the lost souls,
  unloved and unknown,
And to keep praying for them
  until they're Your own ...
For it's never enough
  to seek God in prayer
With no thought of others

who are lost in despair ...
So teach us, dear God,
    that the power of prayer
Is made stronger by placing
    the world in Your care.

And pray in the Spirit on all occasions
with all kinds of prayers and requests.
With this in mind, be alert and always
keep on praying for all the saints.

~ Ephesians 6:18 NIV ~

Not what you want but what God wills

Do you want what you want when you want it?
  Do you pray and expect a reply?
And when it's not instantly answered,
  do you feel that God passed you by?
Well, prayers that are prayed in this manner
  are really not prayers at all,
For you can't go to God in a hurry
  and expect Him to answer your call.
Prayers are not meant for obtaining
  what we selfishly wish to acquire,
For God in His wisdom refuses
  the things that we wrongly desire ...
And don't pray for freedom from trouble
  or pray that life's trials pass you by.
Instead pray for strength and for courage
  to meet life's dark hours and not cry
That God was not there when you called Him
  and He turned a deaf ear to your prayer
And just when you needed Him most of all
  He left you alone in despair.
Wake up! You are missing completely
  the reason and purpose of prayer,

Which is really to keep us contented
   that God holds us safe in His care ...
And God only answers our pleadings
   when He knows that our wants fill a need,
And whenever our will becomes His will
   there is no prayer that God does not heed.

For this reason, since the day we
heard about you, we have not
stopped praying for you and asking
God to fill you with the knowledge of
his will through all spiritual wisdom and
understanding.

~ Colossians 1:9 NIV ~

No prayer goes unheard

Often we pause and wonder
when we kneel down to pray –
Can God really hear
the prayers that we say?
But if we keep praying
and talking to Him,
He'll brighten the soul
that was clouded and dim –
And as we continue,
our burden seems lighter,
Our sorrow is softened
and our outlook is brighter.
For though we feel helpless
and alone when we start,
A prayer is the key
that opens the heart,
And as the heart opens,
the dear Lord comes in
And the prayer that we felt
we could never begin
Is so easy to say,
for the Lord understands
And He gives us new strength
by the touch of His hands.

What is prayer?

Is it measured words that are memorized,
Forcefully said and dramatized,
Offered with pomp and with arrogant pride
In words unmatched to the feelings inside?
No, prayer is so often just words unspoken,
Whispered in tears by a heart that is broken,
For God is already deeply aware
Of the burdens we find too heavy to bear ...
And all we need do is seek Him in prayer
And without a word He will help us to bear
Our trials and troubles, our sickness and
sorrow
And show us the way to a brighter tomorrow.
There's no need at all for impressive prayer,
For the minute we seek God He's already
there.

Your Father knows what you need,
before you ask Him.

~ Matthew 6:8 NASB ~

The power
of prayer

The prayer of a righteous man is powerful and effective.

~ James 5:16 NIV ~

Prayer is powerful. It is one of the strongest forces of energy in the world. It can alter one's outlook: Hatred changes to love, misfortune to blessing, despair to joy, confusion to clarity; ruffled waters become still. Indeed, prayer can change one's life.

Anywhere is a place of prayer if God is there

I have prayed on my knees in the morning,
I have prayed as I walked along,
I have prayed in the silence and darkness,
and I've prayed to the tune of a song.
I have prayed in the midst of a triumph,
and I've prayed when I suffered defeat –
I have prayed on the sands of the seashore
where the waves of the ocean beat.
I have prayed in a velvet, hushed forest
where the quietness calmed my fears –
I have prayed through suffering and heartache
when my eyes were blinded with tears.
I have prayed in churches and chapels,
cathedrals and synagogues, too,
But often I had the feeling
that my prayers were not getting through.
And I realized then that our Father
is not really concerned where we pray
Or impressed by our manner of worship
or the eloquent words that we say.
He is only concerned with our feelings,
and He looks deep into our hearts
And hears the cry of our souls' deep need

that no words could ever impart.
So it isn't the prayer that's expressive
or offered in some special spot –
It's the sincere plea of a sinner,
and God can tell whether or not
We honestly seek His forgiveness
and earnestly mean what we say,
And then and then only God answers
the prayers that we fervently pray.

The Lord has heard my cry for mercy;
the Lord accepts my prayer.

~ Psalm 6:9 NIV ~

The house of prayer

Just close your eyes and open your heart
And feel your cares and worries depart.
Just yield yourself to the Father above
And let Him hold you secure in His love.

For life on earth grows more involved
With endless problems that can't be solved,
But God only asks us to do our best –
Then He will take over and finish the rest.

So when you are tired, discouraged and blue,
There's always one door that is opened to you
And that is the door to the house of prayer,
You'll find God waiting to meet you there.

And the house of prayer is no farther away
Than the quiet spot where you kneel and pray,
For the heart is a temple when God is there
As we place ourselves in His loving care.

And He hears every prayer and answers each
one
When we pray in His name, "Thy will be done."
And the burdens that seemed too heavy to bear
Are lifted away in the house of prayer.

A prayer for healing

I wish I knew some magic words to say
To take your troubles all away,
But at times like this we realize
That God, who is both kind and wise,
Can do what none of us can do,
And that's to heal and comfort you.
So I commend you to His care,
And may He hear your smallest prayer
And grant returning health to you
As only He alone can do.

*And the prayer offered in faith
will make the sick person well;
the Lord will raise him up. If he
has sinned, he will be forgiven.*

~ James 5:15 NIV ~

Prayers can't be answered unless they are prayed

Life without purpose
is barren indeed –
There can't be a harvest
unless you plant seed.
There can't be attainment
unless there's a goal,
And man's but a robot
unless there's a soul.
If we send no ships out,
no ships will come in,
And unless there's a contest,
nobody can win.
For games can't be won
unless they are played
And prayers can't be answered
unless they are prayed.
So whatever is wrong
with your life today,
You'll find a solution
if you kneel down and pray,
Not just for pleasure,

enjoyment and health,
Not just for honors,
prestige and wealth,
But pray for a purpose
to make life worth living,
And pray for the joy
of unselfish giving,
For great is your gladness
and rich your reward
When you make your life's purpose
the choice of the Lord.

On the wings of prayer

On the wings of prayer
our burdens take flight
And our load of care
becomes bearably light
And our heavy hearts
are lifted above
To be healed by the balm
of God's wonderful love.
And the tears in our eyes
are dried by the hands
Of a loving Father
who understands
All of our problems,
our fears and despair
When we take them to Him
on the wings of prayer.

*But they who wait for the Lord shall
renew their strength. They shall mount
up with wings like eagles, they shall run
and not be weary, they shall walk and
not be faint.*

~ Isaiah 40:31 RSV ~

Everyone needs
someone

People need people
and friends need friends,
And we all need love,
for a full life depends
Not on vast riches
or great acclaim,
Not on success
or wordly fame,
But on just knowing
that someone cares
And holds us close
in their thoughts and prayers.
For only the knowledge
that we're understood
Makes everyday living
feel wonderfully good.
And we rob ourselves
of life's greatest need
When we lock up our hearts
and fail to heed
The outstretched hand
reaching to find
A kindred spirit

whose heart and mind
Are lonely and longing
to somehow share
Our joys and sorrows
and to make us aware
That life's completeness
and richness depends
On the things we share
with our loved ones and friends.

*I constantly remember you
in my prayers. Recalling your
tears, I long to see you, so that
I may be filled with joy.*

~ 2 Timothy 1:3-4 NIV ~

Lives distressed
cannot be blessed

Refuse to be discouraged,
refuse to be distressed,
For when we are despondent,
our lives cannot be blessed.
For doubt and fear and worry
close the door to faith and prayer,
And there's no room for blessings
when we're lost in deep despair.
So remember when you're troubled
with uncertainty and doubt,
It is best to tell our Father
what our fear is all about,
For unless we seek His guidance
when troubled times arise,
We are bound to make decisions
that are twisted and unwise,
But when we view our problems
through the eyes of God above,
Misfortunes turn to blessings
and hatred turns to love.

Let your wish become a prayer

Put your dearest wish in God's hands today
And discuss it with Him as you faithfully pray,
And you can be sure your wish will come true
If God feels your wish will be good for you ...
There's no problem too big or question too small –
Just ask God in faith and He'll answer them all –
Not always at once, so be patient and wait,
For God never comes too soon or too late ...
So trust in His wisdom and believe in His word,
No prayer's unanswered and no prayer's unheard.

*If you ask anything in
my name, I will do it.*

~ John 14:14 RSV ~

The key

Though we feel helpless
and alone when we start,
A prayer is the key
that opens the heart,
And as the heart opens,
the dear Lord comes in
And the prayer that we felt
we could never begin
Is so easy to say,
for the Lord understands
And He gives us new strength
by the touch of His hands.

*I pray that out of his glorious riches he
may strengthen you with power
through his Spirit in your inner being,
so that Christ may dwell in your hearts
through faith.*

~ Ephesians 3:16-17 NIV ~

Listen in the quietness

To try to run away from life
is impossible to do,
For no matter where you chance to go,
your troubles will follow you –
For though the scenery's different,
when you look deep inside you'll find
The same deep, restless longings
that you thought you left behind.
So when life becomes a problem
much too great for us to bear,
Instead of trying to escape,
let us withdraw in prayer –
For withdrawal means renewal
if we withdraw to pray
And listen in the quietness
to hear what God will say.

*My soul thirsts for God, for
the living God. When can I
go and meet with God?*

~ Psalm 42:2 NIV ~

God's presence in prayer

Seek the Lord and his strength,
seek his presence continually.

~ Psalm 105:4 RSV ~

Often in the quiet and solitude of prayer, a calm and a reverence develop within and God's presence is felt. Equally appreciated are the moments during an act of loving kindness when the presence of God is experienced. Brief, fleeting, but unforgettable, are those seconds when time and the world stand still as the presence of our God is sensed.

Put your problems in God's hands

Although it sometimes seems to us
our prayers have not been heard,
God always knows our every need
without a single word,
And He will not forsake us
even though the way is steep,
For always He is near to us,
a tender watch to keep.
And in good time He will answer us,
and His love He'll send
Greater things than we have asked
and blessings without end ...
So though we do not understand
why trouble comes to man,
Can we not be contented
just to know it is God's plan!

*And he said, "My presence will
go with you, and I will give you rest."*

~ Exodus 33:14 RSV ~

My God is no stranger

God is no stranger
in a faraway place –
He's as close as the wind
that blows 'cross my face.
It's true I can't see
the wind as it blows,
But I feel it around me
and my heart surely knows
That God's mighty hand
can be felt every minute
For there is nothing on earth
that God isn't in it –
The sky and the stars,
the waves and the sea,
The dew on the grass,
the leaves on a tree
Are constant reminders
of God and His nearness,
Proclaiming His presence
with crystal-like clearness –
So how could I think
God was far, far away
When I feel Him beside me
every hour of the day,
And I've plenty of reasons

to know God's my Friend,
And this is one friendship
that time cannot end.

*Greater love has no one than this, that
he lay down his life for his friends.*

~ John 15:13 NIV ~

My garden of prayer

My garden beautifies my yard
and adds fragrance to the air,
But it is also my cathedral
and my quiet place of prayer.
So little do we realize
that the glory and the power
Of Him who made the universe
lies hidden in a flower!

*O Lord, our Lord, how majestic is your
name in all the earth! You have set
your glory above the heavens.*

~ Psalm 8:1 NIV ~

Thy will be done

Only through sorrow
do we grow more aware
That God is our refuge
in times of despair,
For when we are happy
and life's bright and fair,
We often forget
 to kneel down in prayer,
But God seems much closer
and needed much more
When trouble and sorrow
stand outside our door,
For then we seek shelter
in His wondrous love,
And we ask Him to send us
help from above.
And that is the reason
we know it is true,
That bright, shining hours
and dark, sad ones, too,
Are part of the plan
God made for each one,
And all we can pray
is "Thy will be done."
And know that you

are never alone,
For God is your Father,
and you're one of His own.

*God is our refuge and strength, an
ever-present help in trouble.
Therefore we will not fear, though the
earth give way and the mountains fall
into the heart of the sea.*

~ Psalm 46:1-2 NIV ~

Enfolded in His love

The love of God surrounds us
Like the air we breathe around us –
As near as a heartbeat,
As close as a prayer,
And whenever we need Him,
He'll always be there!

*The Lord is faithful in all his words, and
gracious in all his deeds.*

~ Psalm 145:13 RSV ~

The mystery of prayer

Beyond that which words can interpret
or theology explain,
The soul feels a shower of refreshment
that falls like the gentle rain
On hearts that are parched with problems
and are searching to find the way
To somehow attract God's attention
through well-chosen words as they pray.
Not knowing that God in His wisdom
can sense all our worry and woe,
For there is nothing we can conceal
that God does not already know.
So if we kneel in prayer in His presence
we'll find no need to speak,
For softly in quiet communion,
God grants us the peace that we seek

For God alone my soul waits in silence.

~ Psalm 62:1 RSV ~

Now I lay me down to sleep

I remember so well this prayer I said
Each night as my mother tucked me in bed,
And today this same prayer is still the best way
To sign off with God at the end of the day.
And to ask Him your soul to safely keep
As jou wearily close your tired eyes in sleep,
Feeling content that the Father above
Will hold you secure in His great arms of love.
And having His promise that if ere you wake
His angels reach down, your sweet soul to take,
Is perfect assurance that, awake or asleep,
God is always right there to tenderly keep
All of His children ever safe in His care,
God's here and He's there and He's everywhere.
So into His hands each night as I sleep
I commend my soul for the dear Lord to keep,
Knowing that if my soul should take flight
It will soar to the land where there is no night.

*He will cover you with his feathers, and
under his wings you will find refuge; his
faithfulness will be your shield and rampart.*

~ Psalm 91:4 NIV ~

What more can you ask?

God's love endureth forever –
what a wonderful thing to know
When the tides of life run against you
and your spirit is downcast and low.
God's kindness is ever around you
always ready to freely impart
Strength to your faltering spirit,
cheer to your lonely heart.
God's presence is ever beside you,
as near as the reach of your hand.
You have but to tell Him your troubles –
there is nothing He won't understand.
And knowing God's love is unfailing,
and His mercy unending and great,
You have but to trust in His promise –
God comes not too soon or too late.
So wait with a heart that is patient
for the goodness of God to prevail,
For never do prayers go unanswered,
and His mercy and love never fail.

*Give thanks to the Lord, for he is
good. His love endures forever.*

~ Psalm 136:1 NIV ~

A part of me

Dear God, You are a part of me –
You're all I do and all I see,
You're what I say and what I do,
All my life belongs to You.
You walk with me and talk with me,
For I am Yours eternally,
I cannot dwell apart from You –
You would not ask or want me to,
For You have room within Your heart
To make each child of Yours a part
Of You and all Your love and care
If we but come to You in prayer.

As you have heard from the beginning,
his command is that you walk in love.

~ 2 John 6 NIV ~

God, are you there?

I'm way down here –
You're way up there.
Are You sure You can hear
my faint, faltering prayer!
For I'm so unsure
of just how to pray –
To tell You the truth, God,
I don't know what to say.
I just know I'm lonely
and vaguely disturbed,
Bewildered and restless,
confused and perturbed,
And they tell me that prayer
helps to quiet the mind
And to unburden the heart,
for in stillness we find
A newborn assurance
that Someone does care
And Someone does answer
each small, sincere prayer.

Let us draw near to God with a
sincere heart in full assurance of faith.

~ Hebrews 10:22 NIV ~

God bless you and keep you in His care

There are many things in life
we cannot understand,
But we must trust God's judgment
and be guided by His hand.
And all who have God's blessing
can rest safely in His care,
For He promises safe passage
on the wings of faith and prayer

By faith Abraham, when called to go to
a place he would later receive as his
inheritance, obeyed and went, even
though he did not know where he was
going.

~ Hebrews 11:8 NIV ~

To know

To know beyond belief
that Someone cares
and hears our prayers
provides security for the soul,
peace of mind and joy of heart
that no earthly trials,
tribulations, sickness, or sorrow
can penetrate ...
For faith makes it wholly possible
to quietly endure
the violent world around us,
for in God we are secure.

*The steadfast love of the Lord never
ceases, his mercies never come to an
end; they are new every morning;
great is thy faithfulness.*

~ Lamentations 3:22-23 RSV ~

For you, a prayer
that God will
keep you in His care

Prayers for big and little things
Fly heavenward on angels' wings.
And He who walked by the Galilee
And touched the blind and made them see
And cured the man who long was lame
When he but called God's holy name
Will keep you safely in His care,
And when you need Him, He'll be there.

Then you will call upon me ... and I will
listen to you.

~ Jeremiah 29:12 NASB ~

In hours of
discouragement

Sometimes we feel uncertain
and unsure of everything –
Afraid to make decisions,
dreading what the day will bring.
We keep wishing it were possible
to dispel all fear and doubt
And to understand more readily
just what life is all about.
God has given us the answers,
which too often go unheeded,
But if we search His promises
we'll find everything that's needed
To lift our faltering spirits
and renew our courage, too,
For there's absolutely nothing
too much for God to do.
For the Lord is our salvation
and our strength in every fight,
Our redeemer and protector,
our eternal guiding light.
He has promised to sustain us,
He's our refuge from all harms,
And underneath this refuge

are the everlasting arms.
So cast your burden on Him,
seek His counsel when distressed,
And go to Him for comfort
when you're lonely and oppressed.
For in God is our encouragement
in trouble and in trials,
and in suffering and in sorrow
He will turn our tears to smiles.

The eternal God is your refuge, and
underneath are the everlasting arms.

~ Deuteronomy 33:27 NIV ~